LISTEN
DESIGN
INSPIRE

MATTEO BIANCHI'S CREATIVE JOURNEY

BY SIMON HAMILTON

Published by
Filament Publishing Ltd
16, Croydon Road, Beddington,
Croydon, Surrey CR0 4PA
+44(0)208 688 2598
www.filamentpublishing.com

ISBN 978-1-912635-12-2

© Simon Hamilton & Matteo Bianchi Studio 2018

All Rights Reserved
No portion of this work may be copied without the prior written permission of the publishers

The right of Simon Hamilton & Matteo Bianchi to be identified as the authors of this work has been asserted by them in accordance with the Designs and Copyrights Act 1988

Special thanks to the very talented photographers for capturing Matteo's projects so well over the years.

Juliet Murphy - www.julietmurphyphotography.com
James Balston - www.jamesbalston.com
Mark Weeks - www.markweeks.com

Printed by IngramSpark

Dedicated to all of those who believed in me.

Thank you to those people who have given extra support to Matteo and myself.

"On Matteo, whom I have known for more than 12 years now when he was still working at an advertising agency. We met at a time when he was ready to make the big leap: changing direction in his creative career and create his own design studio.

I have seen Matteo grow from a small practice in East London, making impressive first steps, with fresh ideas and elegant choices.

He has certainly grown and matured over the last years and his style and approach still bear the same freshness. Playing with the unexpected in his compositions, his thought process remains clear and purposeful.

I hope that he will choose to keep these core values in his repertoire and keep surprising the world with great signature pieces".

**Christos Passas B Arch (Hons)
AA Grad Des Dipl, ARB, ETEK,
Associate Director
Zaha Hadid Architects, London**

INTRODUCTION

Meeting Matteo, over 10 years ago in Hoxton Square, has led me to develop a genuine respect and curiosity about his work and approach. I was excited and apprehensive when I decided to write his story. Such a responsibility. This book is not simply about Matteo's transformation from Marketing to the world of Interior Design over the past decade, but more about what inspires and drives someone and how they get through it.

From nothing, Matteo has created a design studio with a reputation for elegance, quality and quirkiness. I feel lucky to have been allowed such unlimited access, which has brought me closer to Matteo. I hope what I have discovered keeps you turning the pages, as I know that there is a lot more to come.

Have a look for yourself.

CONTENTS

HELLO, I'D LIKE YOU TO MEET MATTEO BIANCHI	8
HOW DID MATTEO GET FROM VENICE TO PARIS?	9
VENETIAN CHILDHOOD	10
TEACHING A NEW GENERATION	14
HOW DID WE MEET?	17
HOW DOES MATTEO WORK?	19
RESIDENTIAL PROJECT CASE STUDIES	27
Vera Avenue, Grange Park, London	29
Sloane Court, Chelsea, London	39
COMMERCIAL PROJECT CASE STUDIES	47
Ella Di Rocco, London – Wine MediSpa	49
Brooklins Models, Bath - Office	61
PRODUCT DESIGN CASE STUDIES	69
Juliette Desk	71
Acorn Light	81
Baffo Light	89
Muffin Pouffe	95
THE SECRET OF MATTEO'S SUCCESS	101
WHAT NEXT?	103
ABOUT THE AUTHOR	111

HELLO, I'D LIKE YOU TO MEET MATTEO BIANCHI

HOW DID MATTEO GET FROM VENICE TO PARIS?

It's late January 2018, and I'm in Paris standing next to Matteo Bianchi on an exhibition stand. His excitement is infectious as he is about to unveil the new lifestyle collection his practice in South London, Matteo Bianchi Studio, has created. Only 3 years ago this little-known Italian designer from Venice hadn't even imagined being an Art Director for an International brand. I'd like to tell you more about how he got here and what happened on the way.

Matteo has been designing interiors for the past 10 years in the UK and Internationally. As someone who has boundless energy, I'm feeling humbled by his endeavours in such a short time span. My own career has been a varied and long haul one unfolding over the last 30 years. As you'll soon realise, exploration, food and travel all play a big part in Matteo's story.

The new brand called BABOON has been designed in-house by Matteo and his team for Italian manufacturers GIPRINT. I'd not heard of this company either, but as I learn by spending time with Matteo, he has a knack for finding and building relationships with a diverse range of people and companies.

The Baboon range is certainly accessible to everyone as he was keen to produce something that appealed to all age groups and budgets. This is no Ikea as the quality is much higher, but it could certainly have mass appeal. We will find out later why Matteo has a lot of respect for the famous Swedish brand.

Let's take a cautious little step back in time to find out about his journey to this Parisian launch. In 2017, Matteo's studio was working on several projects. There was a mixture of residential, commercial and product projects on the go, so there is a natural buzz in the studio. Energetic and fun, but always focused on producing what really resonates with the brief and more importantly with his client. Some 'Out of the park' ideas get discussed and then rationalised and kept (if they make sense). Sounds like a thorough process.

As ever, Matteo is focused on getting these projects right, but he also wanted to complete them to meet and sometimes surpass the client's requirements. How do you achieve that whist trying to bring up a young family? I think Matteo's wife Rebecca, deserves a big mention here as his best supporter, firm but fair critic and genuine soulmate.

VENETIAN CHILDHOOD

Matteo's curiosity and creative routes started with his childhood, which began in Venice in November 1975. Growing up as the first son in a native Italian family, Matteo learnt to be grateful for his parents' lessons in integrity, humility and hard work. With an enterprising and practical father Attilio and a naturally bright and organised mother Daniela, Matteo had the sort of stable upbringing so many would wish for.

Matteo grew up in Lido, which is a unique island amongst the 118 islands as it has cars and bikes instead of the infamous canals. He says that unknowingly, during his childhood, he absorbed the art, architecture and culture that were around him. He was lucky enough to have such rich and diverse surroundings as his neighbourhood.

Throughout Matteo's childhood he had strong family influencers. A little different to those you see on Instagram, but no less important. His uncle was a builder, his granddad a carpenter and his father a handyman. Being surrounded by builders has helped him understand how they think, talk, communicate and act. He can talk their language in every sense, which is so valuable when working on a project. Up to the age of 15 years old, Matteo was an only child, but he always wanted a brother. His brother Gianluca arrived in 1990, which was a dream come true for Matteo.

GROWING UP

After High School, Matteo went to Padua. Like so many kids he worked during the Summer months. The glamorous hotels needed extra waiters during the Venice Film Festival, so he got a job at the Excelsior Hotel. Excited and smartly dressed in an Emerald green uniform, he joined the other perky waiters standing in line along the red carpet as several famous Hollywood actors arrived. He remembers fondly that Jack Nicholson picked him out of the line like a Corporal inspecting his soldiers, and said, 'Buena sera' as he walked down the red carpet. This was an important moment in this young man's life. Something clicked and it was then he realised that there was so much more to discover outside of Venice. For the rest of the Summer, he worked as a lifeguard, but he knew this wasn't the life he wanted. Seeing a way out by travelling the world, Matteo entered a competition for a Scholarship in Sweden, which he won. It started in September 1997 and lasted for 9 months.

ESCAPING THE ISLAND

Returning to the Lido Island in September 1998, Matteo felt trapped. He had seen what was out there. His Swedish experience had given him an appetite that he wanted to satisfy. He had developed a taste for travel and learning, so he quickly looked for another scholarship. This time it was to Boston, in the USA.

Once this was completed in July 1999, Matteo returned to his native Venice. He decided to finish University so he could be free. With some money, from a small inheritance, he wanted to go back to the USA. He was fascinated by the way they did things over there. Marketing was very different.

Once the scholarship was up, he reluctantly headed back home again. He applied for several jobs including Benetton, Alitalia and Ikea.

The latter had a long and complex selection process, but he was one of 10 graduates selected because of their high potential. Matteo was 25 years old and in his prime. Ikea decided to invest in these 10 people for the future. Matteo flourished at Ikea. As Ikea's office was in Milan, he could legitimately leave his island life.

Ikea were keen to train the managers of the future at their Italian Headquarters. "The way they understand Branding, Visual Merchandising and Consumer behaviour is exceptional". Once the training and launch were completed, his only option was to be on the shop floor, but he was adamant that wasn't for him. The only other option was to return to Ikea's Swedish Headquarters, which would have meant being in a remote village with few friends. Frustrated, but not defeated, he decided to resign and take the big step of moving to London.

LONDON CALLING

His desire to escape and take control of his life led him to the big smoke. He took the bold decision to sell his car and go to London. He arrived in the capital on 6th January 2004. He only had £4,000, a pressure cooker as cooking was part of his family upbringing, a coffee machine (he is Italian after all) and a laptop.

Daniel was the only friend he knew from Kindergarten that was already living in London. Luckily, he offered him accommodation for 2 weeks. Initially scraping by as so many people do, Matteo worked as a waiter as his English was now much better, but with an American accent. This was a problem as it meant that he couldn't understand English people.

By March that year, his money had almost run out, but resourceful as ever he found a job as a Junior Account Manager with the agency DDB. It was a culture shock of the highest order as it was such a corporate environment with a pace of 100mph. DDB had oil clients and coordinated with 14 European countries so it was high pressured and very stressful. This really couldn't be what he had travelled across Europe for leaving behind beautiful and cultured Venice? Something had to change and fast.

TEACHING A NEW GENERATION

With a feeling of disappointment, but still very driven, Matteo decided that he had to have a plan to ensure he really had a long-term future. A friend was promoted to a job in Manchester and she said that she required a Manager. To boost his income, he went to live up North for a year where it was a lot cheaper than London. He managed to save money for a year and take the steps to finally change his career and plan for the future.

Matteo started his plan by researching several areas that were of interest to him. He took a course in Shiatsu massage, another in Reflexology and he also looked at Interior Design. From his research and childhood enjoyment of drawing, he decided to embark on a part-time course to test his skills and interest. He found the 10-week course at Central St Martins was ideal. He was now 29 years old and very conscientious and determined that he wanted to change his career. This was the point when Matteo realised this was going to be his life.

After visiting several Interior Design schools including The Interior Design School in Queens Park, Matteo decided that Chelsea offered the right course for him. The course was intense, but that suited Matteo's determination. During Module 3 at Chelsea, the students were asked to work on a live project so Matteo had to search around for one. Coincidentally this came about through his best friend Daniel whose friend was refurbishing a hotel in Venice. This was Matteo's introduction to Max Costa, his first client. A larger than life character with a big heart and an appetite to match.

The last and more complicated Module 3 at Chelsea ran from January to April 2007. Matteo went to visit Max in Italy and landed the project as he had proved his scheme was much better than the local architect. This was the perfect opportunity for Matteo to make his mark. He grabbed it with both hands.

At this point, Matteo brought me into work with him, as he wanted to reassure Max by getting an experienced professional on board. "It was an amazing way to work with another designer".

It was an ideal project with an international perspective. Using his Marketing and Accounting training Matteo worked together on costs, planning the budget, workload and timing. It was a fixed price, but Max had the benefit of two designers for the price of one.

Fast-forward to the summer of 2009 and Matteo got another break. His first residential project. A friend living in Lagos, Nigeria, had a wealthy friend who was very frustrated with his Interior Designer. It seemed that the designer didn't understand the client and vice versa. As dedicated as ever and keen to make a good impression, Matteo met his new client on New Year's Day at the client's house just off the Kings Road in the heart of Chelsea. Within a month, he was appointed to redesign the house.

Matteo's relationship with Chelsea continues as he teaches in London and Dubai on a regular basis. Having a chat with some of the people that know Matteo has given me a better insight into who he is:

"He researched everything thoroughly and sat in on a class. He showed his commitment and decisiveness. He brought another dynamic and we had an immediate connection, as Matteo was extremely passionate and dedicated. He is absolutely driven and found that he was very good at materials, so much so, that he sourced things not seen before in Module 1. He brought in amazing samples such as recycled yoghurt pot worktops, which made him stand out. I asked him to come and teach as he was good at materials and he was a natural. He is clearly very passionate. I asked what else are you passionate about and he said lighting, so he now runs the lighting course. Once he began teaching he also took student crits. In recent years, he has been teaching less to concentrate on the business. Now and then he takes on Interns into his studio from Chelsea, two of whom have learnt from him and set up their own design business together".

Lyndall Fernie
Short Course Leader, Chelsea College of Arts, London

"My first encounter with Matteo was to support a Student Open Day. Matteo is the first tutor to have been on the course then run one. He has become a fantastic ambassador, giving students confidence to launch their careers. Matteo was in the perfect position to work on 'How To Start Your Interior Design Business'. He is very diligent and good at identifying opportunities. He is always evaluating himself and seeing where he can give back, like public speaking courses. He has always been a solid tutor and incredibly reliable. He is always clear about what he can and can't do and I have never seen him without a smile. A real networker, he is always recommending people. Matteo has a very generous spirit. Support for other people comes naturally to him. He is always looking out for other people's interests. A lot of people would benefit if they had his attitude".

Roberta Bonfield
Short Course Manager, Chelsea College of Arts, London

"What I have respected most with Matteo is his professionalism. He has an openness and willing personality. He shares and engages in the wider community of education. He has business intelligence, which has allowed him to connect dots that are not immediately obvious. I trust his instinct. He has managed to straddle the sensitivity around learning and being commercially sensitive to the future development. Matteo possesses uniqueness and he will contact me and suggest someone. He has a natural generosity".

Kate James
International Business Director, Chelsea College of Arts, London

"He's enthusiastic and passionate about the industry. Being from a Marketing background gave him a questioning approach. As an Interior Designer, he's adventurous in terms of lighting and furniture, out of not being able to find the right products. The hotel project in Venice was the first one that made him stand out. He sees the importance of networking and is a good listener. Being a family man now, he has a new perspective on his work ethic and getting a balance. He has an investigative approach and is always curious. Matteo took the student crit last year and showed that he has a very encouraging point of view. Matteo wants to make a difference in the industry".

Iris Dunbar
Director, The Interior Design School

HOW DID WE MEET?

In March 2007, there was an advert posted in Gumtree for an Interior Designer to work for my design company: Simon Hamilton Interior Design Ltd. At the time, I was an Interior Designer with over 15 years of working in the design industry, mainly on commercial and residential projects. I lived in East London and worked from a studio near London Bridge station, long before it became associated with the buzz it has now and years ahead of the Shard. Matteo met me for a coffee in Hoxton Square at the Blue Note café where he announced at our initial meeting that he could bring a project to me. I thought he was just being cheeky and very ambitious. However, I was proved wrong as Matteo was true to his word and our relationship blossomed from there onwards.

Matteo worked with me as a freelancer for a few weeks. I had much more experience, running a studio, so for the first time; this experience gave Matteo a tangible vision of what he should aim for. We had a very good working relationship. As it was a small office, it gave him the idea to run his own studio rather than work in a bigger practice. He experienced the whole process. We shared a common understanding and passion for design. Having the privilege to see how a company is run, gave Matteo the idea of how he could run his own company.

HOW DOES MATTEO WORK?

LISTEN DESIGN INSPIRE

INITIAL CLIENT MEETING

Matteo always likes to meet the client in person so that he can get to know them in their own space. Listen, listen, listen. That's the mantra Matteo repeats time and again. Matteo insists that he first listens to his client. For every residential project, he asks them how they live? How do they interact with family, guests and friends? How do they relax? What is their routine? Importantly, what are their passions? This gives a real insight into how a client thinks of themselves and where they are. Do they like reading, cooking, parties, listening to music or watching films? Are there any special requirements e.g. storage, audio-visual, acoustics, ergonomics, ventilation, environmentally, space saving, special equipment and historic? The latter refers to items or habits that may have to be incorporated into the new design. It's also important to establish if there are any priorities. The aim is to come away with a very clear Design Brief in his mind. Matteo likes to summarise a project into key words, as these are easy shorthand when discussing the project with the team.

Matteo's first big commercial project in the UK was for Location, Location, an Estate Agency in the centre of Upper Street, Islington. As several estate agents occupy the same section of this packed High Street of Islington, it was vital to make a statement with lasting impact. The client gave the rather abstract Design Brief "I like Apple minimization with an industrial hint typical of All Saints". The project even won the prestigious '**International Property Award for Best New Office 2015**'. Matteo attributes this to the client being brave. He felt he could trust Matteo fully and had the courage to go all the way. This project represents something memorable and a distinctive progression of the concept to reality. The office interior was one of the first living walls in a commercial space

What Matteo really loves about his job is his connection with his clients. For one client, he researched the Chinese culture and found out that birds bring prosperity. Peacocks are very important as well as round tables. By carrying out this intensive and detailed research he ends up having a much deeper connection with his clients as he can understand what matters to them. Matteo knows that his residential Italian clients will demand a very sociable island for their Kitchen so they can chat around preparing food.

LISTEN DESIGN INSPIRE

"Tripping the Light Fantastic" was the summary name given to a project for a gay couple in Clerkenwell who had lots of parties and were very sociable. Will and Grace would have approved. They didn't cook, but the Kitchen still had to look good and function properly. They were keen to show off their success. There was no need for a big Dining Table, but a bar style surface with seating for up to 4 people was requested. This enquiry came through an estate agent whom Matteo had contacted. He was getting good at networking. Matteo says that

working for a commercial client is interesting in different ways, as you must listen even more, because there is a brand, a target and a purpose for the project. The business has a purpose and there is a target market and business strategy. Listening is crucial, so he can understand what they like. The client will speak on behalf of the company and interpret the brand. Sometimes the task can include repositioning the brand and helping that company to become more established in their market sector.

WHAT DOES THE DESIGN PROCESS REALLY INVOLVE?

FEE PROPOSAL

Once Matteo feels that they can work together then he will prepare a Fee Proposal for his client. To ensure that there is a clear and proper understanding of the process of Interior Design, Matteo explains in absolute detail the way he and his team work and all the stages involved. The Fee Proposal is a detailed written document with Standard Terms and Conditions. In advance of commencing any work, Matteo will request a deposit from his client of 50% of the Creative Presentation or Concept Stage. In paying this in advance, the client shows their commitment and integrity. As with any good business, Matteo recognises that this is a two-way relationship and vital that this is respected from the outset. The design team will put in a lot of effort and passion at this part of the process so that they can really deliver a concept, which is original, exciting, practical and achievable within the time, budget and regulations. The Fees are divided into 4 clear stages so it makes the whole process visible and easy to understand from the outset. Clarity and integrity is key with Matteo and how he works with his clients.

CREATIVE PRESENTATION

The Creative Presentation will start with the team putting together ideas based upon Matteo's meeting and the Design Brief. At this stage, the team have not met the client directly, so excellent communication from Matteo is essential to ensure the team knows everything that is relevant and the project scope and priorities. The client's expectations must always be well managed, so a site meeting with the client is key to discuss ideas in real terms. This sometimes means that Matteo will need to travel abroad. Matteo's team carries out a survey of the space, as it is the best way to understand the space.

The Creative Presentation also involves mood boards, fabric swatches, proposed space planning, lighting ideas, sketches, material samples and finishes which are suggested for the client. This is a critical stage for any designer, as it shows how the designer is interpreting the requirement and developing the design brief. The overall look and feel is established at this point. The best ideas are presented. There is no deliberate house style, but by default, clients will have an expectation based on the portfolio and previous projects.

DRAWING PACKAGE

This is the production of accurate drawings required to build, details of items and construction, lighting plans and information, Mechanical and Electrical layouts using Computer Aided Design software such as Vectorworks and AutoCAD (otherwise known as CAD) drawings. This is valuable information, which is shared with other professionals such as Architects, Building Regulations departments, Quantity Surveyors, Planning Officers, Furniture Makers, Building Surveyors, Engineers and Lighting Consultants, Joinery Companies as well as other suppliers where required or necessary.

F, F & E

Fittings, Finishes and Equipment known as F, F & E, are a crucial and complex process of research, sourcing, selection and specification gathering. Matteo carefully develops long-term relationships with his suppliers so that he has a trusted network. Timing is critical and it can be stressful as it is dependent on other people, companies and suppliers in the main. This takes time and commitment from all parties. There have been hiccups along the way, when he has trusted a supplier to deliver a product as specified, only to be let down. For this stage, an Interior Designer is only as good as the relationships with suppliers. Matteo will only work with suppliers whom have personally met even if that entails a meeting abroad. He goes to the showroom and / or factory and does not trust them until they have a personal meeting. If the client has a supplier then the responsibility is taken on by them not the studio.

The F, F & E is handled in two distinct stages as follows:

A - Shopping List
B - Sourcing

A - The Shopping List is where the studio will research all the items and provide the client with the full details.

B - Sourcing is a more involved process as the studio will research all the items but also be responsible for purchasing, delivery and installation to the project.

Matteo also operates an open book to reassure clients about how their money is spent. He has trade discounts and offers clients the discount with an administration fee on top. On average, the client will spend less than if they bought the items themselves directly so there is an incentive to use this arrangement. Transparency is key and non-negotiable. As an interior designer offering to purchase goods, this has a risk of liability, hence Liability Insurance is important and a requirement as a member of British Institute of Interior Design (BIID).

PROJECT CO-ORDINATION

This is the part of the process, which involves site visits, delivery of materials and quality checks throughout the project. This is crucial to the success of every project as it is when the implementation of the concept becomes reality. It relies on excellent and clear communication with all those involved. With such a collaborative effort, the design team are dedicated to making sure the process goes as smoothly as possible.

There will always be challenges in any project, but these can be overcome by co-ordinating information and making informed decisions, on behalf of the client with their best interests at heart. Matteo and his team uphold very high standards of all they produce in the studio, whether it's a sketch, mood board, presentation, technical drawing, schedule or instruction. All this information is vital to manage the project from the 2-Dimensional to become a 3-Dimensional reality on site.

LISTEN DESIGN INSPIRE

RESIDENTIAL PROJECTS

CASE STUDIES

LISTEN DESIGN INSPIRE

CASE STUDY 1
VERA AVENUE, GRANGE PARK, LONDON
2017

"Residential projects can take longer, but they are rewarding as you can become part of the family. As you need to click from the start so that a client can trust you, it's important they feel comfortable. I like the intimacy this brings to a project. It's very fulfilling".

Located in the outer zones of the capital, Grange Park is in the quiet suburbs of North London. Just take the A10 to Winchmore Hill and a few turns later, you'll soon be there. An established and middle class neighbourhood, electric gates and manicured lawns abound. The clients met Matteo through his BNI networking group. He sure has determination, as he's been attending business Breakfasts every Tuesday at 6.30am for the past 8 years. No overnight sensation story here! These family focused clients Stella and Peter had not worked with an Interior Designer before, but Matteo's naturally personable manner was an instant comfort to them as there was a lot to do. The clients had an interesting brief.

"The clients like to have a lot of friends and family around at the weekend, which means having 15 to 20 people to visit at any one time. It was a challenging prospect accommodating so many people comfortably, whilst making sure the design was classy and practical. This was a complicated space, but the client wanted to follow our advice as their initial wish list was too long. It would have cluttered the whole house. We decided a small rear extension across the full width of the house was required as it was crucial for the space to breathe".

"I designed everything in the property, which included the Kitchen. As the clients really loved cooking, they shared the same passion, so it became even more personal. I ask lots of key questions; do you use one or two ovens? What sort of food do you like to cook? Asian, French, Greek? I get into the real details. What's the feeling you want to get out of the Kitchen? Is it important that it is very practical or is elegance more important to show off?

"I'm a self-confessed lighting freak', so I always insist there are at least 3 lighting scenarios; Task, General and Mood Lighting. With this you are sure to have the right light for your needs. I like to add an LED strip at high level where possible to provide discrete background lighting".

"A big new Breakfast bar was designed as it created a perfect preparation area, but also allowed the client to serve her food buffet style, which was the client's preference. A manmade material was used for this in a neutral tone with a bronze painted toughened glass splashback for added contrast and texture. In terms of finishes, the client liked the herringbone wooden floor that was proposed. They decided on the dark stained oak finish that gave the subtle elegance the client was after".

"The clients really trusted us and felt comfortable with us. The client let the studio choose all the finishes and manage the budget. They followed my lead all the way to the end. It's been an amazing journey".

LIVING ROOM BEFORE

KITCHEN BEFORE

LEFT: LIVING ROOM AFTER
BELOW: ENTRANCE HALL FROM LIVING ROOM

LISTEN DESIGN INSPIRE

KITCHEN AFTER

KITCHEN AFTER

KITCHEN AFTER

DINING ROOM AFTER

MATTEO BIANCHI'S CREATIVE JOURNEY

HOME ITALIA MAGAZINE FEATURE
JANUARY 2018

The project has been hailed in Italy to the degree that Home Italia magazine has featured it on the front cover for its December 2017 – March 2018 edition. It's the first time Matteo has been on a cover, which he found quite emotional.

MB
Matteo Bianchi

Founded in 2007 in London ...ign and inspire. Founded in 2007 in London ... of creative and talented designers, Matteo ... distinguished international Interior ...ssfully developed more than 110 ... is to create bold and stylish ...eir clients at its best. ... every each one, ...ng an elegant, ... force

Ascoltare, fare design, ispir... 2007 e composto da ... Bianchi Studio è un... design d'interni che ha ulti... in tutto il mondo. La l... audaci e ricchi di sti... committenti. Co... lavoro sanno ... i suoi sogni ... Matteo ... dietro ...

LISTEN DESIGN INSPIRE

CASE STUDY 2
SLOANE COURT, CHELSEA, LONDON
2011

Matteo rose to the challenge for this project in the prestigious area of Chelsea. Known for its titled and high net worth residents, as well as glamorous shopping and nightlife, it was going to be a demanding project.

A traditional period Pied-a-Terre apartment with 3 bedrooms, the interior was very basic, magnolia walls, cream sanitary ware, plain Kitchen and boring carpet throughout. No real statement and very dated, which provided a blank canvas to create the mix of "East meets West" the Chinese clients were looking for. Matteo used traditional elements with a mix of eclectic style and a contemporary touch. Above all the clients wanted a luxury family home, that would function well for their two daughters, but also work at night for entertaining friends. Like any project it had its challenges, but getting to know the client was the best way to reassure them their expectations could be managed.

"As we weren't changing the interior structurally, we didn't have to worry about the status of the building as such, but as it was an apartment we obviously had strict building control. We wanted to respect the age and look of the property though and keep period features such as the sash windows and balcony doors. It suited the style we were trying to achieve".

The space is composed of two smaller children's bedrooms, off the Hallway, which leads into a Dining space, which is very open and airy. This connects four ways – into a neat modern Kitchen, then into the impressive Living Room, which is the biggest of the spaces with balcony doors. There is an elegant Family Bathroom and the 'hotel like' Master Bedroom, with luxury En-suite Shower Room, all on one floor.

Matteo used materials such as cherry wood furniture and hand painted wallpaper to keep the traditional Eastern feel and introduced contemporary solid oak flooring from Europe. The team explored strong colour palettes and mixed in modern furniture to add a twist. They designed many bespoke pieces such as the soft furnishings and fitted wardrobes.

Because of the layout, the Dining Room is certainly the heart of the property with its full wrap of beautiful, vibrant, hand painted silk wallpaper which was very expensive. The design and logistics of the hand painted wallpaper needed to be measured to the millimetre, so that it matched up on every edge. To overcome this Matteo, ensured the wallpaper was applied with another contractor on hand to repaint the pattern so it matched precisely. This distinctive wallpaper cleverly covers the frameless doors.

Designing the children's rooms was an important part of the brief as the clients wanted to share the luxury with their children. Matteo wanted to give the two girls rooms a look that echoed their personalities. The older girl has a funky and fun room with exciting wallpaper, a spacious desk and a magnetic white board – great for a teenager.

"It was exciting to work with international suppliers. The brief was a new and inspiring challenge for the studio, but we learned a lot about combining styles". In all, the project took 12 months from Matteo's first meeting to completion. When it was finished the clients said, "Wow that's amazing". The result was better than they expected.

BATHROOM BEFORE

BATHROOM AFTER

LEFT: MAIN RECEPTION ROOM
BELOW: ENTRANCE HALLWAY AND DINING SPACE

YOUNG DAUGHTER'S BEDROOM

LISTEN DESIGN INSPIRE

COMMERCIAL PROJECTS

CASE STUDIES

LISTEN DESIGN INSPIRE

CASE STUDY 1
ELLA DI ROCCO WELLNESS MEDISPA
CHELSEA, LONDON
2018

Ella Di Rocco is the realization of Matteo's client, Dr. Anna Brilli's lifetime dream and the latest project in the Studio's portfolio. Working on one of the coolest projects he has embarked on during his 10-year rise is very exciting and challenging for Matteo's studio. Ella Di Rocco is London's first Wellness Medispa offering wine bath therapies. Based in Fulham Road, the concept involves bathing yourself in red wine, as it is full of antioxidants and very good for your skin. This treatment used to be very common in ancient Rome.

Arranged over 2 levels, the spa is a hidden gem with unique treatments available. The client wanted it to be the first in London and she has created Ella Di Rocco as a space for relaxation, rejuvenation and inspiration. An implantologist, a maxillofacial surgeon, and accomplished business woman, Anna has travelled and worked around the world, reflecting her rich global experiences in the diverse Ella Di Rocco offering.

There is one in central Italy and another similar spa in Switzerland. If it works well the owner will franchise the concept.

There are 3 private Treatment Rooms with calming colours, soft towels in abundance and infinitely dimmable lighting. From a former retail unit to the reality of 2018, has taken 12 months of discovery, exploration, research, prototyping and innovation as the project was highly technical from the outset. It incorporates some avant-garde technology including equipment directly from NASA.

The full treatment begins by entering the elegant store at street level and taking the staircase at the back to the lower ground level. There are bespoke fittings and features throughout, which were developed with the client for their specific purpose very much in mind. Even the bold black and white patterned wallpaper is unique to Ella Di Rocco. Once at the lower level, you enter the private spa decorated with deep green walls, black and white floor tiles, treatment beds and relaxing dimmed lighting.

Once undressed and prepared, you are given a gentle body scrub with grapes. Then you take a shower, whilst your bath of red wine, water and grapes is prepared. After you immerse yourself in the deep bath of red liquid for a set period, you take a step out to experience a full body massage on one of the bespoke loungers. Following this you can sit on the leather sofa to recover. For this last stage, your feet are treated to a soothing bath whilst you have a drink of red wine. All treatments are non-invasive and natural to the extent that carefully selected vegan beauty products are also available to buy. This was a very tricky project to design because of the limited space to accommodate all that was required. The access was difficult and the lower ground had to be extensively tanked to ensure it is watertight. Ella Di Rocco represents the essence of Matteo's approach, as he listened very carefully to his client to produce a unique design which has more than inspired the owner Anna, to see what is possible and consider developing other Ella Di Rocco branches.

AN INITIAL CONCEPT SKETCH FOR ELLA DI ROCCO

RIGHT: MAIN STAIRCASE
BELOW: ELLA DI ROCCO RECEPTION

LISTEN DESIGN INSPIRE

BELOW: TREATMENT ROOM
RIGHT: SPA TREATMENT ROOM

RIGHT: WINE BATH DETAIL
BELOW: SPA TREATMENT ROOM

LEFT: THE SPA TROLLEY PREPARED FOR TREATMENTS
RIGHT: WINE BATH PREPARED

LISTEN DESIGN INSPIRE

CASE STUDY 2
BROOKLIN MODELS, BATH, SOMERSET
2016

The client for Brooklins Models, Pietro Marini had never worked with an Interior Designer before, but they became friends after meeting Matteo from an introduction by Matteo's wife Rebecca. Pietro was impressed with Matteo's straight forward, no bull**t attitude. From a fellow Italian, it was refreshing Pietro says. The owner bought the business located in the UK, because it was the last of its kind, as most of the competitors have moved abroad. The owner is a car enthusiast with more than 300 cars in his garage. He felt passionately about preserving this business in the UK.

Started a year before Matteo was born, in 1974 in Canada, the company has become the world-leading manufacturer of scale model cars. Pietro Marini was appointed as Director by the new owner, it was the right time to upgrade the brand so that every company CEO would have a Brooklins model on their desk. The existing building did not reflect the values and quality of products they manufactured in this niche market. It was dark and unwelcoming so they decided to have a new Reception area to meet and greet clients. The brand identity was developed based on the era of the cars, which is mainly the 1940's and 1950's.

The Brooklins models are handcrafted with the same loving care and attention as a jeweller would to produce custom pieces. Because of the beauty of the product, the company needed to give the offices real status. "Elegant but not posh" said Pietro. The project progressed and was spot on with the client's expectation. The work was carried out mostly at the weekend so as not to disturb production. During the work in progress some changes were made. Matteo was good on directing their decisions to the best choice.

Matteo's attention to detail really paid off. The space is much more welcoming and a true representation of this niche manufacturer in a specialist market. The use of simple materials that provided the right style and feel that reflects the quality of the brand meant the space is designed to a high specification.

There is a mirrored bespoke Reception desk to greet you as you arrive with a clutch of Baffo lights, suspended over the desk. The full range of the car models is neatly displayed in large cases with internal lighting. There are also jewel-like dark wood trimmed boxes recessed into the Reception wall with moody lighting to show off extra special models. The Brooklins name stands proud and two comfortable looking button-back leather armchairs provide welcome rest.

The result: a happy client and a very successful project, which has been awarded the prestigious **'Best Office Interior South West UK 2017' by the International Property Awards.**

LISTEN DESIGN INSPIRE

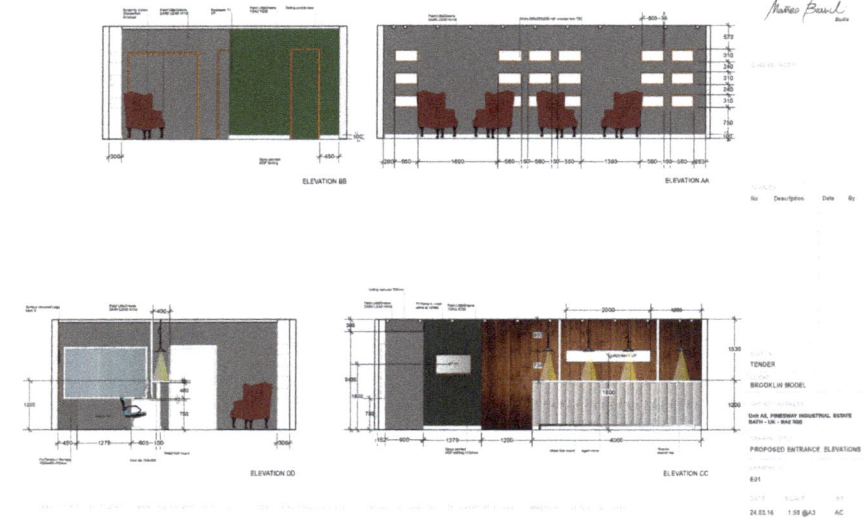

RECEPTION DESIGN DRAWINGS

BROOKLINS NEW RECEPTION

BROOKLINS NEW RECEPTION

BROOKLINS NEW RECEPTION DISPLAY CASES

BROO

LISTEN DESIGN INSPIRE

PRODUCT DESIGN

CASE STUDIES

LISTEN DESIGN INSPIRE

CASE STUDY 1
JULIETTE DESK, TISETTANTA
2016

Only 2 years ago, at the London Design Festival Matteo saw lots of lighting companies showing their products. Gallotti & Radice whom he knew well because of specifying their products, asked him to present a talk. It was to be an inspirational talk about trends in lighting. It was at this event that he happened to meet Fabrizio Pedrazzani who was the Showroom Manager and son of the owner of Tisettanta. He showed him the Acorn light and they chatted about design trends. By coincidence Matteo had just placed an order for a project in Portobello Road. The Art Director had just passed away, so Fabrizio wanted to bring in new designers and a fresh approach.

Fabrizio needed to focus on dining and working and storage sideboards for the end of September/mid-October, so Matteo was happy to discuss the possibilities. He visited the showroom and he understood the style like a fashion house. A week later he went to Dubai for a teaching assignment. Luckily, he could stay on an extra day and soak up some sun, but mainly as he needed some headspace to think clearly and dedicate to this collection. On a visit to a beach near the famous sail building the Burj al Arab, with magazines, a sketchpad and pencils he could free his mind and relax. This is where he developed the sketches that were to become the very footprint of the Juliette Desk. He presented these to the team on his return to London. One design was safe and another a little more adventurous.

Matteo's connection with Fabrizio was not only that they were both born and raised in Italy, but they shared a similar perspective. They literally speak the same language and both enjoy being highly professional. "I like to do product design as you get to know the people behind the company. You must share the same values and goals. It gets very personal, but it's still business in the end. There is a certain level of risk, but mainly for the manufacturer. Sure, it can be stressful ensuring the shareholders get their return on investment and there is a lot of adrenalin".

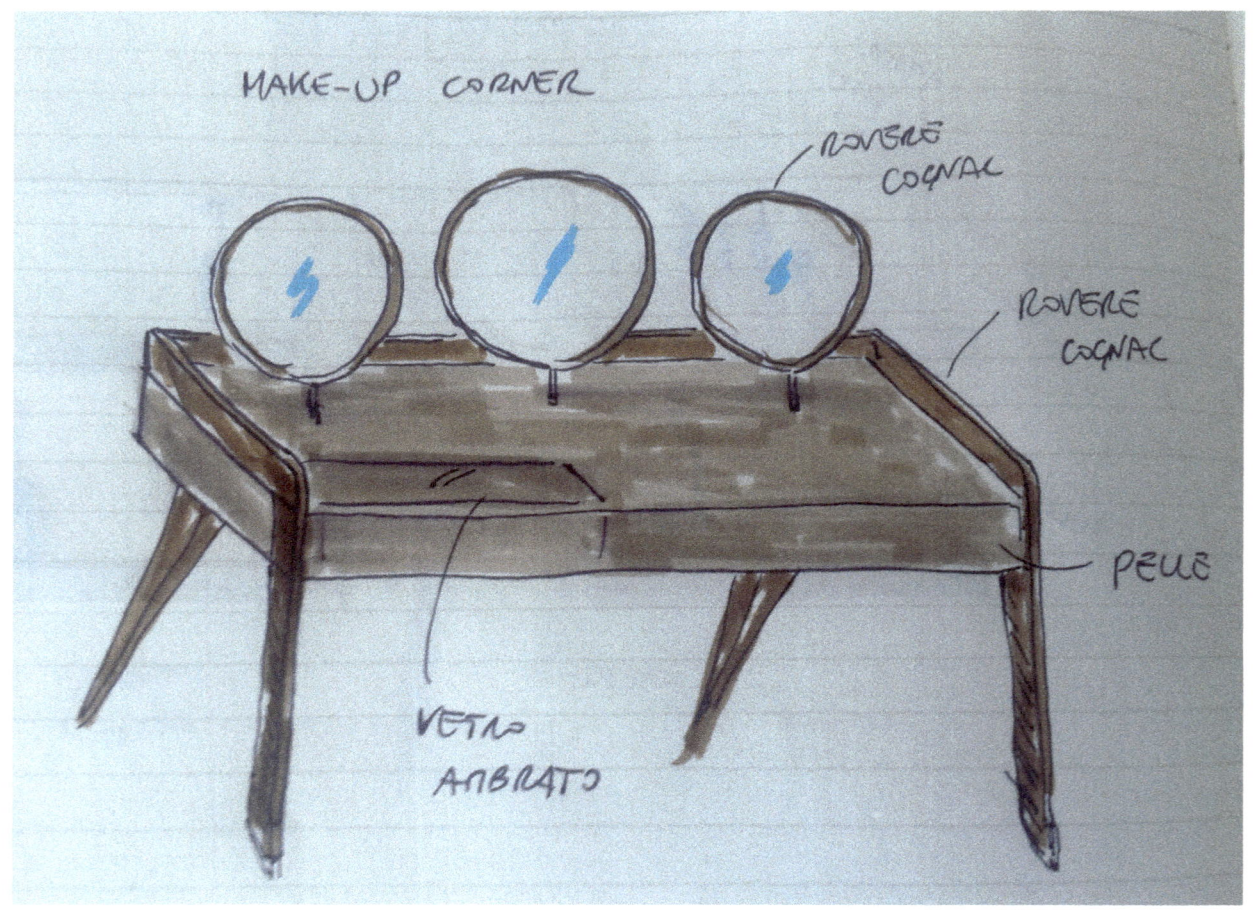

Perfect for Matteo who likes a bit of stressful energy to keep going. It was crucial to get the next collection right from the start otherwise he may as well just pack up now.

"The design is important, but the relationship is very intimate and you get to know the people very well. Trust is a long-term process and takes time to build trust and digest".

With Matteo's approach, he understands people and how brands live and develop through their heritage. He will go and see the production line and learn about the history. "You cannot be a product designer without listening" he says. Matteo is always thinking about what's missing from the market. Does this product have profitability? Does it match the brief? Would my peers buy it?

In December, Matteo went to Milan to show Fabrizio's father the designs. He didn't like the first ideas. Right there and then Matteo sketched in front of him and developed the shape of Juliette desk. Symmetry and asymmetry at the same time. During that meeting, together they created the design and talked about the fine details.

The launch date was agreed as April 2017. He went back to Italy a few times and produced a more formalized design in January 2017.

He went back each month to choose the leather and visited the factory. "The secret of product design is the relationship with the manufacturer. If you don't get along it's not going to go anywhere. It feels like they are inviting you into the family when you go to a company. The designers are like members of the family with shared values".

They finally chose all the finishes, but it all happened at the very last minute. The infamous Salone del Mobile in Milan was due to open on Tuesday 4th April. On the previous Thursday, Matteo went to the factory, but there was only the carcass in mdf, not even spray-painted. Alarm bells were ringing as this was cutting it close, however by Monday morning, the finished desk was delivered and installed on the stand. Matteo remembers how emotional he felt to see it complete for the first time.

"Product design is not subjective. The real judge is the market. How well it is perceived by press and ultimately sales". The Juliette desk is the first product to be launched for Tissetanta. Matteo has since been commissioned to extend the Juliette range and develop more products for 2018.

FACTORY VISIT

LISTEN DESIGN INSPIRE

LISTEN DESIGN INSPIRE

FACTORY VISIT

DESK MOCK UP

JULIETTE FURNITURE DETAIL

LISTEN DESIGN INSPIRE

CASE STUDY 2
ACORN LIGHT, PENTA
2015

The Acorn light was produced out of sheer frustration, which has become a common theme with our Italian creator. Matteo's desire to find the right product for his projects has driven him forward more than any designer I know. With so many designers creating products, it's easy to think that these ideas become products overnight with the minimum of effort.

On one of Matteo's annual pilgrimages to Salone Del Mobile in 2014, he observed the design trends, as part of ongoing research, but also for his Chelsea teaching. As Milan often exhibits trends 1 or 2 years ahead of the main market, what you see is often significant. He noticed a very strong trend for making the Bathroom a cosy place like the Living Room and Bedroom had been for years. There was a massive message from the market that you can make the Bathroom into a beautiful space. It made sense, as we now all want to spend time away from the high stressed metropolitan lives we lead. All the effort was being invested in the Bathroom, which is where we find ourselves escaping to. In the UK there are very strict and sensible regulations about the use and position of any electrics in a Bathroom. All light fittings have to be IP rated (which is the resistance to the ingress of moisture or water to the fitting) to IP44 or above, even if they are far from a water source. Different regulations exist in Europe, but the product was intended for international use. Returning to London, Matteo rejoined his team to work on a big development in Gloucester Place. In the presentation for the scheme there was a view of one bathroom with two basins. Although they liked the scheme, their main comment was "the only thing missing was a pendant over the basins".

Matteo told the client about the trend he had just seen in Milan, so naturally his client asked where could he find such a fitting. Matteo simply said "Leave it to me. Trust me, I'll sort it out." Approaching a few industry friends, Matteo's idea struck a chord with Alberto Pavanello. A trusted long time friend and colleague, Alberto had great industry connections especially with Penta, one of the leading Italian lighting manufacturers. They were prepared to take on the concept and had faith in making Matteo's vision a reality.

Marble was being used in different ways. Concrete too was seen in products, so Matteo decided to challenge convention and mix glass with concrete. Why not? It's not just for skyscrapers and floors. Some designers were even experimenting with wrapping marble.

"There seemed to be a trend for functionality," Matteo recalls of 2014. Within a relatively short 6-month period, Penta had produced 10 fittings for all the apartments so it was a win-win situation for all concerned. The client had the first ones and the research and development costs were covered, because of the bulk first order for the project. In a beautifully crafted nutshell that, ladies and gentlemen is the story of how the Acorn light was developed and born.

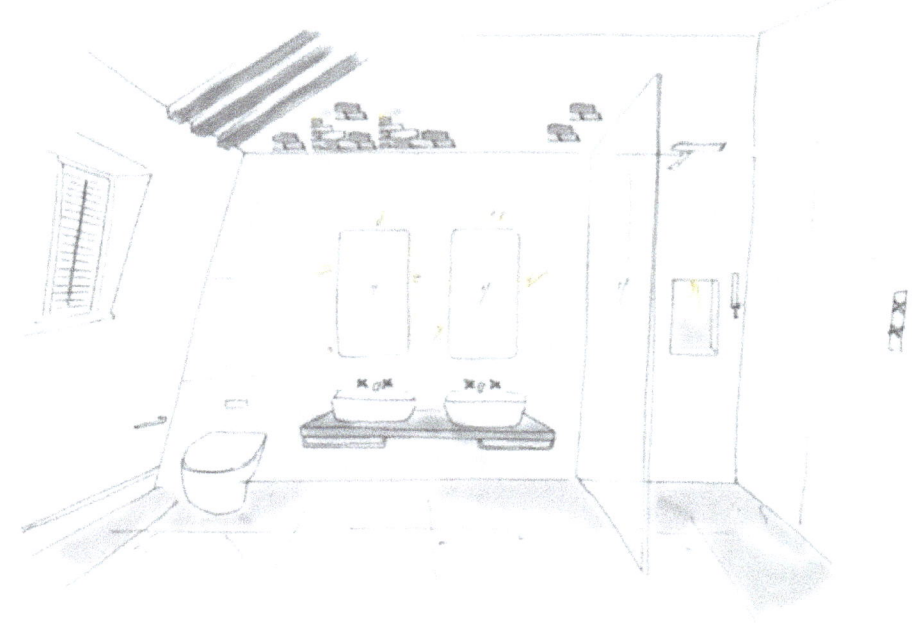

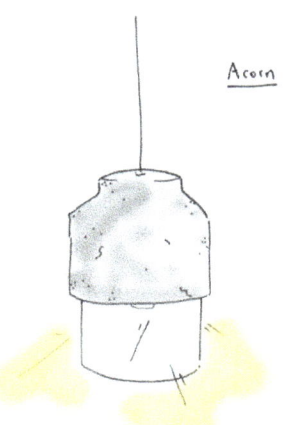

Acorn

TRYING OUT AN ACORN PROTOTYPE

MATTEO BIANCHI'S CREATIVE JOURNEY

BELOW: THE ACORN CLOSE UP
RIGHT: ACORN IN SITU

CASE STUDY 3
THE BAFFO LIGHT, ITALAMP
2012

In 2012, London was about to host the Olympics for the first time since 1948, so there was an immense feeling of national pride and enthusiasm in the air. Matteo fed on this energy and saw a gap in the market. Pendant lights were very popular and being used by lots of designers. Through Matteo's lecturing in Dubai about trends, he had become like a shark, able to detect something in the water that others would miss. Metals were on trend and not just for the Olympic torch that travelled across the nation. The problem was, there were no pendants that could give you directional light and ambient light simultaneously. Matteo wanted to create a fitting that had both features within the same fitting. On a quest to find products for another project, Matteo visited Lewes, and saw a trombone, which he bought.

The trombone's long and slender shape had the perfect opening at one end to provide space for a lamp. This was the inspiration he was looking for. Matteo likened the shape to a cat's face with whiskers and named the light Baffo, which is Italian for whiskers or moustache. After drawing several sketches to develop the idea he put the design aside.

By chance a potential new project came up in Clissold Park, North London for a developer. It involved designing 10 luxury apartments for a past client. They were going to be unfurnished, but decorated with lighting. The Baffo light seemed like the perfect design and an opportunity to use the product in volume.

RIGHT: BAFFO LIGHTS INSTALLED
AT M&M PROPERTY

Matteo knew he had to have the right company to produce the design. For a long time he had admired the products of an Italian manufacturer, Italamp and he wanted to do something with them. He approached them with the design concept and they loved it. Over the next 12 months he developed the Baffo lighting range with their team.

The product sells well and is regularly specified, giving a small amount of annual royalties. It's available in different finishes – black nickel and gold nickel.

Baffo had its official launch at Salone del Mobile in 2017 and Matteo is now developing a family of products around the Baffo product range.

LISTEN DESIGN INSPIRE

BAFFO PENDANT LIGHTS

CASE STUDY 4
MUFFIN POUFFE, MATTEO BIANCHI DESIGN STUDIO
2011

The Muffin pouffe came about after Matteo was feeling blue when a personal relationship came to an end. It's certainly a natural reaction to want to comfort yourself, but most people, myself included would have bought or made a cake not made one from wood and leather!?! He was fascinated with this as it had such contradictory elements. A soft overflowing top and ridged base. Matteo embarked on making his first product so he could learn the manufacturing process first hand. He funded the whole process himself and learnt the hard lessons and setbacks of prototyping, testing, detailing, materials, manufacturing, production and distribution.

The final result is a versatile and playful product range that can be an occasional seat, used around a dining table or a statement piece in both commercial and residential settings. By removing the cushion, the Muffin pouffe reveals hidden storage space; unexpected, functional and refined. The 'ingredients' are selected by the customer from a range of beautifully handcrafted solid wood bases, Italian prime cut leathers and buttons.

LISTEN DESIGN INSPIRE

MUFFIN POUFFE LAUNCH

Matteo Bianchi

MUFFIN POUFFE GROUP SHOT IN SHOREDITCH

MUFFIN POUFFE WITH WHITE LEATHER LID

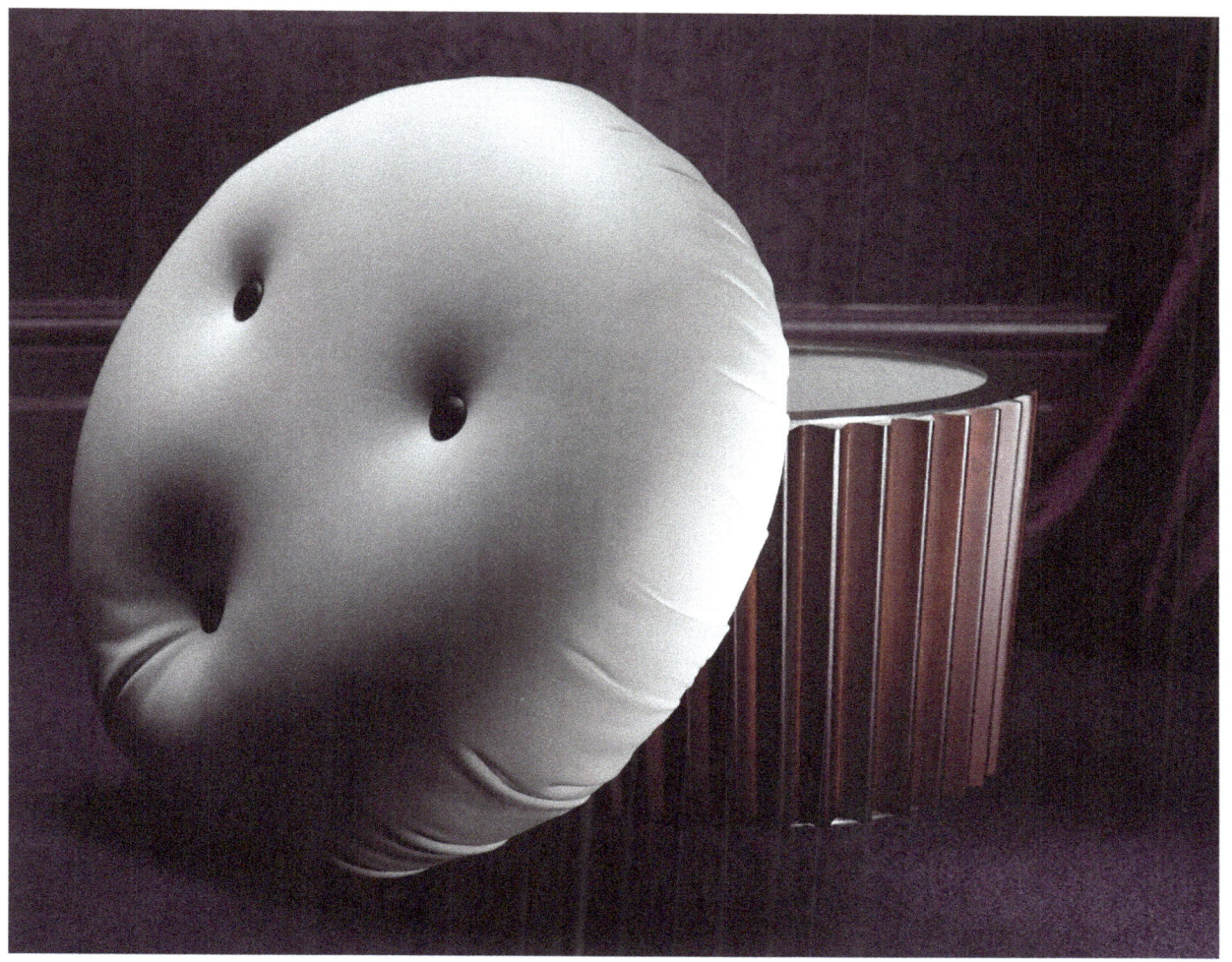

THE SECRET OF MATTEO'S SUCCESS

To answer this ultimate question, I need to bring you back to Paris where we began. The launch of Baboon Lifestyle at Maison et Objet in Paris, sees the start of a new era in Matteo's evolution as a designer. He has put in the hours, got up (very) early for several years on the trot, been focused, driven and dedicated. That's what it takes!

But that's not all. If it was simply that, then we'd all be exhibiting at a major international design show and launching a new brand with a pioneering Italian manufacturer. Now that puts it into perspective. Not so easy eh? There is a lot of talent that isn't just about being imaginative and creating Instagram-ready interiors. It's also about a positive attitude and the ability to really connect and work well with people.

Communicating his ideas with energy and passion has been at the heart of what Matteo stands for. He has lots of ideas, which as Matteo would say, "are always bubbling away". That might drive some people off course, but he can park some of those ideas for later, research others and turn the rest into real projects.

It's clear to see that not being constrained by the conventions of an Interior Design degree has its advantages. The writer's background is more conventional and has been an influence on how I've thought about my own career progression. Matteo went straight out there and did whatever it took to get himself set up as soon as he could. He wanted to take charge of his own future. To shape it and influence it, without looking to anyone else for approval.

Perhaps it's his background of growing up into a hotbed of culture like Venice? What he has produced so far is set to become something, which is atypical of most Interior Designers venturing into product design.

The mantra Listen, Design, Inspire is the thread for all that he creates. From the very first meeting with a client or the seed of an idea, Matteo has his ears and eyes open to possibilities. Spending the past 12 months with Matteo, I have learnt that he possesses an innate desire to innovate and create, and to do so with charm and a sense of fun. He is straight talking and will tell clients how it is without any unnecessary fluff or fuss. This is what makes him stand out as a designer with integrity and a long future of designing for a variety of lucky private and commercial clients from across the globe.

LISTEN DESIGN INSPIRE

WHAT NEXT?

MATTEO BIANCHI'S CREATIVE JOURNEY

A WORLD OF POSSIBILITIES...

LISTEN DESIGN INSPIRE

THE END

ABOUT THE AUTHOR
SIMON HAMILTON BA(Hons) FRSA

A specialist of Interior Design, Simon Hamilton has completed projects internationally from concept through to handover for private and commercial clients. His creative work includes numerous projects for the Workplace, Retail, Hospitality and Residential sectors.

With over 25 years in the design industry, including running his own Interior Design business for more than 10 years, Simon's ability to lead, design, communicate, manage and deliver projects is well proven. Working as a Consultant of Design recruitment for several years, Simon has also gained valuable expertise within this sector for the UK, European and Asian markets.

He strongly values Design Education and teaches a variety of Interior Design Courses for University of Arts, London at the Chelsea College campus in addition to being a Visiting Tutor at The Interior Design School, London.

Twice elected to the role of International Director for the British Institute of Interior Design (BIID) from 2010 – 2014, Simon attained Board level. He was responsible for creating, developing and managing relationships outside the UK on behalf of the BIID. He has represented Interior Designers through presentations to audiences across diverse cultures and attitudes in Europe, Japan, Canada, Russia, India and the USA.

Simon continues to be inspired by attending major design events around the world. Through this exposure to design, he creates and hosts reviews for architects, designers, students, manufacturers and design publications.

Since 2014, Simon has been on the judging panel for the International Property Awards and is a Fellow of the Royal Society of Arts.

As part of Simon's portfolio career, he is Studio Director for Matteo Bianchi Design and for 2017, he was selected as a brand ambassador for Decorex to celebrate their 40th Anniversary in September.

simon@simonhamilton.me
www.simonhamilton.me
+44(0)7973 541 637

LISTEN DESIGN INSPIRE

www.ingramcontent.com/pod-product-compliance
Lightning Source LLC
Chambersburg PA
CBHW042026100526
44587CB00029B/4312